Holy Disruptors:

A Christmas Season Devotional

Journey with Biblical Women

By

Jamie Coles Burnette, M.Div., M.A.

Independently Published,

Jamie Coles Burnette, ©2021

Copyrights

Holy Disruptors: A Christmas Season Devotional Journey with Biblical Women by Jamie Coles Burnette, M.Div., M.A.

Scripture quoted by permission. Quotations designated (NET) are from the NET Bible® copyright ©1996, 2019 by Biblical Studies Press, L.L.C. http://netbible.com.

All rights reserved.

Scriptures are taken from the New Century Version®. Copyright © 2005 by Thomas Nelson. Used by permission. All rights reserved.

Published by "Jamie Coles Burnette Ministries"

Printed in the United States of America

U.S. Copyright © 2021 No. 1-10874992761
ISBN: 978-0-578-30160-0

Table of Contents

Acknowledgments 4

Preface 5

December 24th: Mary, Mother of Jesus 7

December 25th: Shiphrah & Puah 11

December 26th: Naomi 15

December 27th: Huldah 19

December 28th: The Prophet's Widow 23

December 29th: Rhoda 27

December 30th: Tamar (Mother of Zerah & Peres) 31

December 31st: Eve 35

January 1st: Daughters of Zelophehad 39

January 2nd: Vashti 43

January 3rd: Lois & Eunice 47

January 4th: Mary, Sister of Martha & Lazarus 51

January 5th: Leah 55

January 6th: Hagar 59

Author's Bio 64

Connect: 66

Acknowledgments

I am eternally grateful to the Triune God,
and my great cloud of witnesses, both living and transitioned,
whose words and deeds of love have formed and encouraged me in this, and every endeavor:

Mom, Jean Coles;

Dad (transitioned), Leander Coles, I;

My husband and life-partner, Elliot;

Pastor ViCurtis Little;

Evangelist Elaine Campbell (transitioned);

Pastor Rose Bess (transitioned);

Apostle Cierra L. Jones

Preface

Grace and Peace this Christmas Season!

This is a time of year that affords us another moment of sacred analepsis and prolepsis– a time of looking backward (analepsis) and forward (prolepsis) in gratitude, wonder, and hope – as we reflect upon both the first and second comings of our Lord Jesus Christ. It reminds us of the inbreaking of God's kingdom into human history in the form of God-made-flesh; and that we look forward in hope to God's inbreaking into human history once again in final joy and victory at Christ's second coming.

Our yearly celebration of the birth of Jesus Christ also invites us to think about the ways that God is ***always*** breaking into human history, even in the most ordinary and mundane of human experiences. This inbreaking of God does not come quietly. Rather, it is often interruptive and disruptive to norms, systems, the status quo, and "principalities, powers, and spiritual wickedness in high places." God shakes what needs to be shaken not only without but within us so that we can experience "righteousness, peace, and joy in the Holy Spirit" (Romans 14:17), which are the true hallmarks of God's Kingdom.

The Biblical women featured in this devotional are part of the "God-story" of God's interruption and disruption of human affairs. "The fact that most of them are named in the Biblical text is itself a disruption of ancient cultural norms where women's voices often meant very little." Their stories of faith, loss, tragedy, and victory make them "holy disruptors": women whose stories remind us of the ways that

God works through the messy, the tragic, and the ordinary to bring about "peace on earth, and goodwill towards humanity," starting with our own lives.

This devotional allows us to journey with these women through this unique and reflective time of year: from Christmas Eve, through the 12 Days of Christmas, up through January 6th, Epiphany Day, which is a day that reminds us of the ways that God has revealed, and is yet revealing God's self to us. Through their stories, it is my sincere prayer that you will experience hope, faith, joy, peace, and transformation as you contemplatively engage with God through these women of Scripture.

This work is a labor of love many years in the making and was inspired by my late, beloved Aunt Elaine. It was born out of a conversation we had long ago regarding creating something to uplift women. While she has gone from labor to reward, her legacy lives on as she served as a holy disruptor in many ways and a catalyst for me to write this book. For that, and so much more, I thank her and all of the women along the way that has inspired me to become the best version of myself and walk in my God-given purpose.

May the Love and Shalom of God be yours in abundance, now, and always,
JLCB

DECEMBER 24th
Mary, Mother of Jesus
"Graced for the Journey"

Background Reading: Luke 1:26-38; 2:25-35

So Mary said, "Yes, I am a servant of the Lord; let this happen to me according to your word." Then the angel departed from her. (Luke 1:38, NET)

Mary's story is one of the most told of Scripture and rehearsed in the Christian faith. Every Advent and Christmas season, we hear the story of this young girl from Galilee who found grace in God's eyes and who would become the mother of the "Son of the Most High."

What is perhaps most captivating about Mary is her faith demonstrated by her willingness to undertake such an incredible task. So much uncertainty and so many changes lay ahead: her body, her reputation, the questions from Joseph and others, not to mention her own questions. But God is always faithful to give us faith-anchors: places and experiences to which we can return in moments of uncertainty and difficulty, and no doubt, Mary would have those moments in parenting Jesus.

One of Mary's faith-anchors was Gabriel's salutation: "Greetings, favored [or graced] one! The Lord is with you." (Luke 1:28, NET). This greeting assured Mary that she was indeed graced for the journey ahead and that the Lord had been and would be with her. Mary would have to hold onto these words when her beloved firstborn son was now a grown man preaching the religiously and politically dangerous message of "The Kingdom of God," putting Himself in the crosshairs of the powers that be. She would have to hold on to these words as she couldn't protect Him from being arrested and killed in a most humiliating and torturous way, and the sword that the prophet Simeon told her about would indeed pierce her very soul.

We, too, will have soul-piercing moments on our journey – especially the journeys that we undertake in total surrender to God's will. Surrender to God's journey for us certainly does not exempt us from pain, sorrow, or suffering. Still, in the surrendering, God is faithful to give us faith-anchors along the way that we have been graced for the journey, and that as the Lord was with Mary, so the Lord is indeed with us.

Prayer: *Faithful God, thank you for my journey. I surrender myself anew to the path that you have laid out before me. I thank you that I am graced for this journey and that You are with me. I may not understand all you are doing, and neither may those around me, but I am committed to trusting You and staying in the process. In moments of discouragement, I pray for reminders of my experiences of your faithfulness to me so that I can move forward in courage. In the Name of Jesus the Christ, Amen.*

Put it into Practice: As a reminder that God has graced you for your journey, every morning this week, as a part of your morning routine, repeat Gabriel's greeting to yourself. Say to yourself in the mirror, or close your eyes and repeat to yourself, "Good morning, favored one! The Lord is with you!." It may seem silly at first, but say it until you internalize it and know it to be true!

Notes

Notes

DECEMBER 25th
Shiphrah and Puah
"Holy Disruptors"

Background Reading: Exodus 1

"So God treated the midwives well, and the people multiplied and became very strong. 21 And because the midwives feared God, he made households for them."
(Exodus 1:20-21, NET)

Shiphrah and Puah: the first Biblical female dynamic duo. Whenever you see two or more women planning something, working together in the Bible, or anywhere for that matter, just know that something ***major*** is about to go down. There is something powerful about women working together that can change and has changed the world, and these two women worked together as holy disruptors to preserve a people.

Being a holy disruptor is more than just a notion – it is a series of brave and bold decisions held together at the core by one major conviction --- the fear of the LORD: the reverential posture of the heart towards the holiness, otherness, and character of God resulting in a worldview and lifestyle that honors God, oneself, and others. This fear of the LORD outweighed the fear of any consequences Shiphrah and Puah might have suffered at the hands of Pharaoh. Shiphrah and Puah's actions were more than saving Hebrew babies, but about paving the way for the liberation of an entire people for and to God.

As for us, this same fear of the LORD includes but goes beyond the awe-inspiring moments of worship that cause us to fall on our faces. It calls to us in our innermost being to act in ways that disrupt wickedness and injustice wherever it is found, uphold the dignity of all persons, and strive for the well-being of others. It beckons us into love for God, self, and others, even at the cost of personal risk and sacrifice. Even more, this holy disruption is not just an interruption of evil and wickedness, but, it is a divine inbreaking of God's Kingdom into human history to bring about wholeness - shalom.

Prayer: *Holy God, we honor You as we are keenly aware that Your eyes are upon us and Your ears are open to our cry. We pray for strength, wisdom, and courage as we endeavor to stand with You for holiness, justice, and righteousness. We ask that the perfect love of God would arise within us and cast out fear that would seek to silence and paralyze us in the moments that being a holy disruptor calls for personal risk and sacrifice. We thank You that You promise to be with us always, and we pray that you would deal well with us in our partnering with You. In the Name of Jesus the Christ, Amen.*

Put it into Practice: Think about what is a "holy disruptor" means to you. What does that look like in your life? What patterns in your mind, your household, family, and community, need to be divinely disrupted? In what ways do you think God may be calling you to be an instrument of God's shalom in these places?

Notes

Notes

DECEMBER 26th
Naomi
"Embrace Your Ruth"

Background Reading: The Book of Ruth

"Stop urging me to abandon you! For wherever you go, I will go. Wherever you live, I will live. Your people will become my people, and your God will become my God... When Naomi realized that Ruth was determined to go with her, she stopped trying to dissuade her." (Ruth 1:16,18, NET)

The story of Ruth and Naomi is a powerful account of two women that had lost everything, but in the end, with God's help and each other, we're able to forge a new path of hope and joy. They had both lost their husbands, but Naomi's pill was doubly bitter: she lost not only her husband but both sons, and with their deaths, seemingly any real prospect of hope. By her own account, Naomi was too old to start over with a new husband and have more children, and she had nothing that she could see to offer her daughters-in-love, Ruth, and Orpah. The best advice she could give them was to tell them to leave her, return home, and start fresh.

Certainly, there will be times when we, too, will be dealt life's bitter pill, but like Naomi, we will also be faced with a decision: to cross over from grief into despair and self-isolation or to accept the Ruth that God has sent. Ruth's name means "companion/friend." By refusing to leave Naomi's side, Ruth was a gift to Naomi even when Naomi insisted. A gift that reminded her that although she had little to offer by society's standards, she still had worth. Ruth's devotion assured Naomi that she was willing to be present in whatever hardship they might face together, that she would listen to Naomi's wisdom and instructions, that she would stay.

No matter how lonely or bitter life becomes for us, God will give us a Ruth who is able to see and will acknowledge our worth. Someone who can look past our portfolios, optics, and bottom lines and value us based on the treasure that lies within. On our part, when God does send our Ruth, we must not push them away. We must recognize and trust the hand of God at work.

As for Ruth and Naomi, because of their mutual trust in each other and God's grace, their bitter cup became a cup of joy once more in which they were both able to partake; and they are a reminder that bitter waters can become sweet again as we embrace the people that God sends into our lives.

Prayer: *Loving God, thank You for Your providential care. Thank you that I have value and worth – precious treasure in this jar of clay. Thank you for the friends, like Ruth, that you have brought and are bringing into my life to affirm and remind me that what I carry is valuable. Help me not to push them away, and in moments of bitterness, remind me that You are able to exchange it for a cup of joy. In the Name of Jesus the Christ, Amen.*

Put it into Practice: Can you think of a time where you served as a Naomi or a Ruth in someone's life? Or can you think of a time when someone served in those roles in yours? In what ways has your life been enriched by that relationship? Do you sense God calling you to function as a Ruth or Naomi in someone's life right now? If so, how?

Notes

Notes

DECEMBER 27th
Huldah
"A Trusted Voice"

Background Reading: 2 Kings 22

> "And she said to them, 'This is what the Lord God of Israel has said: Say this to the man who sent you to me: This is what the Lord has said..'"
> (2 Kings 22:15-16a)

The trajectory of the nation was changing. King Josiah was in the midst of a reform leading the people back to the worship of YHWH. During that reform, while making temple repairs, a scroll of the Torah was found. When it came time to find out the next course of action, the king's advisors didn't look for Jeremiah or some other well-known prophet at the time; instead, they went to the home of Huldah, a prophetess and wife of the king's wardrobe keeper.

While we only hear about her once in the Bible, her contribution to Judah was so vital that she is named in the Biblical text, and the Word of the LORD given through her was recorded. What made her so special?

She was trusted at a crucial time. Interestingly, the king's advisors chose to seek out Huldah of all of her prophetic contemporaries (including the prophet Jeremiah). Scholars have offered up several reasons why Huldah was sought out as opposed to more "well-known" prophetic voices, but regardless of the reason why, the point is, she could be trusted to give the authentic Word of the LORD at an important juncture in Judah's history. The question to us is, Can God *and* our community trust us to be an authentic voice? Have we cultivated life and ministry of integrity that invites trust at crucial moments? People like Huldah aren't called upon because there's no one else to listen to, but they are called upon because they have sown the seeds of integrity and faithfulness over time that gives weight to their voice.

She was not moved by the status of the king. When asked about the Word of the LORD, her initial reply was, "When asked about the Word of the LORD, her initial reply was, "This is what the Lord God of Israel has said. Say this to the man who sent you to me..." What an interesting way to refer to the King of Judah! She did not refer to him by a royal title or even by name, just as "*the man who sent you.*" She starts off by stating that it is **God** who has spoken on the matter. Thus, she places the weight on the Word of the LORD, not on the status of the king. Like Huldah, can God trust us to remain authentic and integral regardless of who seeks us out? As we walk out our callings, will we keep the focus on the Word of the LORD instead of the status of those before whom we are called to stand?

One word stood the test of time. Huldah's prophetic words helped shape the religious trajectory of a nation for a generation, simply because she was willing to be obedient to God and not allow anything to taint her prophetic well. When we release God's words in faith and obedience, they, too, will stand the test of time and go before us into the generations to come.

Prayer: *Holy God, thank You for the power of Your Word. I recognize the weight that words hold and the responsibility You have given me to be a bearer of Your spoken and lived-out Word in my community and the world. I pray for the strength to be unmoved by earthly status, power, or position when I am charged to use my prophetic voice.* May I live a life that engenders trust from my community when they need Your authentic word through me. May I always release Your word in boldness, knowing that it is a seed that will bear fruit in my generation and the generations to come. *In the Name of Jesus the Christ, Amen.*

Put it into Practice: Prayerfully reflect on how you, like Huldah, have or can build trust with the community you are called to serve so that you can be called upon to give an authentic "Word of the LORD" during crucial moments. What actionable steps can you take to grow as an authentic prophetic voice that can be trusted by God and the community?

Notes

_____
_____
_____
_____
_____
_____
_____
_____
_____
_____

Notes

DECEMBER 28th
The Prophet's Widow: "What's in Your House?"

Background Reading: 2 Kings 4

"Elisha said to her, 'What can I do for you? Tell me, what do you have in the house?' She answered, 'Your servant has nothing in the house except a small jar of olive oil.'" (2 Kings 4:2, NET)

The prophet's widow was in a tight spot, to say the least. Her husband, a prophet no less, was dead, and like so many loved ones who are left behind in the wake of a person's death, she was now left with his debts. It was a desperate situation as the creditors were now knocking at her door, threatening to enslave her sons to satisfy the debt. What was she to do?

As a little girl, I remember going with my dad to the IMAX theater – you know, the ones where you feel like you're a part of the movie. I remember watching the movie (about dinosaurs), and the movie felt so real. I got up out of my seat and was scared and felt like I was going to fall. I then looked over at my dad with tears in my eyes and said, "Daddy, I'm scared!" And he said firmly, but calmly, "It's just a movie; sit back down in the chair." While that wasn't the response I was looking for, it was the one I needed. His response didn't coddle me or affirm me in fear. Instead, he took my focus off of how I was feeling and put it back on the reality of the situation: what I was seeing didn't have the power to harm me, and all I needed to do was correctly reposition myself. That's a sermon for another day right there – wink* wink*.

Much like what I learned from my experience in the IMAX, the prophet's widow in the text teaches us what to do when we face potentially panic-inducing situations: go to the right source and obey instructions. She went to the prophet Elisha, who could explain what to do, and she listened to what he said. What is powerful about this story, in addition to the fact that the oil miraculously kept flowing, is that all it took was a small jar of oil to save her and her household from destitution. Elisha asked her a key question, "What have you in the house?" She didn't have to look elsewhere to get what she needed: the solution was at home -- it just took the man of God to draw her attention to it.

When our backs are against the proverbial wall, it is easy to be overcome by fear or panic; one of the greatest problems that fear presents is that it breaks our focus and causes us to lose perspective or fail to see a solution is right in front of us. As I experienced with my own father, God does not affirm us being in a state of fear. God comforts, not coddles. As we seek God and listen to God's voice, God will often draw our attention to an overlooked resource that will help us in time of need -- one that may even seem insignificant at the time. But here's the wisdom and power of God: God has never needed a lot (or, in the case of creation, anything) to work with to get the job done.

So, I encourage you that no matter what you're up against, even when fear tries to overwhelm you, allow God to recalibrate your perspective and show you what solution may be right under your nose. It may be a knack or talent that you haven't used in years. It may be in a magazine article or social media post that inspires you to take a specific action. Nothing is too small to be used when placed in God's hands. What do you have in **_your_** house?

Prayer: *Gracious God, thank you for all that you have invested in me. Help me not overlook any gift, grace, talent, ability, or resource you have entrusted into my hands. In challenging times, help me courageously use what you have given me, as in it is my strategy to overcome. In the Name of Jesus the Christ, I pray, Amen.*

Put it into Practice: When was the last time (if ever) that you took the time to sit and write down your God-given gifts and abilities and reflect on the ways that you have been (or haven't been) putting them to use? Are there any gifts that you have put on the shelf? If so, why? I encourage you to commit the stewardship of your gifts to prayer this week and listen intently to the ways Holy Spirit leads you to awaken, revive, and/or sharpen your gifts.

Notes

_____
_____
_____
_____
_____
_____
_____
_____

Notes

DECEMBER 29th
Rhoda
"Entertaining Angels"

Background Reading: Acts 12:1-17

"When she recognized Peter's voice, she was so overjoyed she did not open the gate but ran back in and told them that Peter was standing at the gate. But they said to her, 'You've lost your mind!' But she kept insisting that it was Peter, and they kept saying, 'It is his angel!' Now Peter continued knocking, and when they opened the door and saw him, they were greatly astonished." (Acts 12:14-16, NET)

Rhoda bore witness through her joyful exclamation that the answer to the believers' prayers was standing right at the door. However, her testimony was dismissed as the ravings of a madwoman. At that time, women's words did not matter, to the point that women were not deemed credible enough to testify in legal proceedings. Unfortunately, honoring the weight of women's words is something that society still struggles with today in many ways.

How many people like Rhoda has God sent into our lives to bear witness to God's love, power, and truth, but because they didn't come from our preferred or expected culture, race, gender, economic status, or share our political or world views that we could not see how God could be at work in and through them? If we're honest, I'm sure we can think of more occasions than we'd like to admit.

Hospitality is one of the most powerful virtues and gifts a person can possess, but it is about more than being willing to invite people over for dinner and games. Hospitality ultimately reveals a posture of the heart that is open to God and the supernatural. Persons who can receive the "other" of *this* world are often prepared to receive the "other" of the *spiritual* world. The writer of Hebrews tells us to remember to show hospitality to strangers, as we could be entertaining angels without knowing it. In an ironic twist, it is interesting that the early believers were more ready to entertain an angel than believe the testimony of a flesh and blood person standing right in front of them.

We should remember that God's truth and power do not rise and fall on whether or not we believe God's appointed messenger, but the question is, how long will we keep "Peter" knocking because we refuse to believe whom God has sent?

Prayer: *Creator God, Who has made all humanity in Your image. Forgive us for the times that we have been dismissive of the least of these in our midst because of fear or ignorance. May the times that we have been dismissed or overlooked make us all the more aware of and compassionate towards those among us whom we and our world have ignored and dismissed. We open our hearts to You, God, and the surprising and unexpected ways that You will choose to speak to us and visit us. We extend our hearts to those You will put in our paths, and we release fear of the other and the unknown to You, in the Name of Jesus the Christ, the One Who became different for us and our salvation, Amen.*

Put in into Practice: This week, practice being more intentionally aware of those whom you encounter. As Holy Spirit leads, engage with someone whom you normally would not. Journal about your encounter and what you experienced and learned about yourself, the person, and God.

Notes

Notes

DECEMBER 30th
Tamar (mother of Zerah & Peres)
The Power of Self-Advocacy

Background Reading: Genesis 38

"...She is more upright than I am because I wouldn't give her to Shelah, my son..."
(Genesis 38:26, NET)

Tamar's story is one of shrewdness and bravery. She had lived through the death of her husband, Er, and a string of failed disappointments and promises. Widowed and childless, her one lifeline to any kind of stability would be through the ancient custom of levirate marriage. If a man died without an heir, the next oldest brother would act as a surrogate to create progeny in the decedent's name (I know. Eek!), which also secured the widow's place in the family. But when the men in the family failed to see to Tamar's security because they were looking out for their own interests, she was left with an uncertain future. Who would look out for Tamar?

Tamar decided that she would not just fade quietly into the background, nor would she continue to allow decisions to be made for and about her. No more broken promises. No more waiting for anyone to deliver on their word. This time, she would advocate for herself and secure her own place in the world and a legacy for her deceased husband, even if it meant acting in ways that were unorthodox and jarring to those in her context and our own contemporary sensibilities.

There are times in life when we, too, will have to go it alone, and with God's help, be assertive, countercultural, and bold in order to see to it that our dignity, worth, and future are honored. While people may prove themselves untrustworthy and disappoint us, we can always trust in the One who promises to never leave us, nor forsake us, and who will give us the strength to find our voice when we need to stand up for ourselves and our future.

Indeed, Tamar's bold actions not only secured a future for her but a legacy that continued on far beyond her lifetime. She ended up giving birth to twins – some theologians say, one child for each broken promise and disappointment – becoming an ancestress of King David. She is one of only four women specifically named in the genealogy of Jesus Christ.

So today, I ask you, what will it take to stand up for *you* and your future?

Prayer: *Faithful God, I thank You that You are the One who is always there. When others are not faithful, You are. I ask for and receive the strength and courage it takes to find and use my voice and stand up for truth, myself, and my God-ordained future, even when it means that I may have to act in unconventional ways. As I advocate and contend for my dignity and my future, may I do it in love, truth, honor, and integrity. In the Name of Jesus the Christ, Amen.*

Put it into Practice: Is there an area of your life where you feel that you've lost your voice and need to speak out or stand up on your own behalf? Write down a few action steps of what self-advocacy in that area would look like, and prayerfully begin implementing them.

Notes

Notes

DECEMBER 31st
Eve
"There is Life After"

Background Reading: Genesis 3-4

"The man named his wife Eve, because she was the mother of all the living."

(Genesis 3:20, NET)

Ah, Eve. The woman who gets blamed in part for this broken world as we know it and for all of the unpleasant parts of being a woman (i.e., labor). Speaking candidly, I wish we could hear more of her voice in the Biblical narratives in Genesis. I wish we could have heard more about her life *before*. You know, before the conversation with the serpent. In her words, I would want to hear her experience of the beauty of the "naked and unashamed[ness]" in her relationship with Adam that we today long for and strive towards. Those walks in the cool of the day with God. The harmony with the earth, sky, sea, and the rest of creation. But, most of our attention is directed towards her life *after*. After her theological discussion with the serpent causes her to mistrust and disobey God. After the fact that life as she knew it would no longer exist.

Like Eve, at some point in life, all of us will make decisions out of fear and mistrust that will cause us to miss the mark of God's best for us. However, Eve teaches us that despite whatever changes, pain, and loss we experience, even those due to our own hands, there is life after. Life after divorce. Life after abuse. Life after tragedy. Life after-- fill in the blank. Genesis 3:20 tells us that Eve's very name means "life" and notice that she doesn't receive this name until *<u>after</u>* her whole world turns upside down. This means that despite her new reality, every time anyone called her name, she would be reminded of the purpose she could still live into and that she could and would still produce and experience life.

Life after is not a life free of consequences, but it is an invitation to experience the grace of God in unexpected and new ways. The grace to accept that things may not be like they once were, but to trust that God is able to make all things new, and to partner with God to forge a new path ahead and to produce new life, even as Eve declared in Genesis 4:1, "With the Lord's help, I have given birth to a man."

Prayer: *God, thank you for my life. I am grateful that nothing in my past disqualifies me from a bright and beautiful future. Thank you that there is yet life in me and for me. I receive the grace and the courage to forge ahead into unchartered territory with You, and I am excited about what my partnership with You will produce. In the Name of Jesus the Christ, Amen.*

Put it into Practice: Take at least 15 minutes and reflect on times that you have experienced God's grace in unexpected ways or times that God has given you a fresh start. Release to God any past decisions or experiences that hinder you from embracing the future God is laying before you. Journal about your reflections, offering God an expression (prayer, song, poem, etc.) of thanksgiving.

Notes

Notes

JANUARY 1st
Mahlah, Noa, Hoglah, Milcah, and Tirzah
(The Daughters of Zelophehad)
"The Courage to Pioneer"

Background Reading: Numbers 27:1-11

"So Moses brought their case before the Lord. The Lord said to Moses: 'The daughters of Zelophehad have a valid claim. You must indeed give them possession of an inheritance among their father's relatives, and you must transfer the inheritance of their father to them.'"
(Numbers 27:5-7, NET)

Being the first to do or stand for something is a mixture of exhilaration and formidability. Certainly, pioneering is never easy, but these five sisters dared to stand before God, Moses, and all of Israel to plead their case for the right to inheritance and a place in their society. It takes a special kind of person to be a pioneer: one has to be brave, patient, and able to push past the contrary voices giving a million and one reasons not to embark upon the God-given endeavor in one's heart. Indeed, these five sisters – Mahlah, Noah, Hoglah, Milcah, and Tirzah – were special people. They had the "stuff" it took to stand up to receive what was theirs, and through their bravery, set a new legal precedent in the nascent Israelite nation. Of the many things we can learn from their witness, here are three that we can learn from their pioneering spirit:

First, they envisioned an existence for themselves that was bigger than their present reality. Yes, they knew the rules, but they saw something more significant and greater. They would not allow their own legacy, security, or their father's name to die out just because he had no sons, and they were willing to exhaust every possible option available to pursue their endeavor. Likewise, suppose we want to accomplish things that others have not. In that case, we must use our imaginations and creativity to envision something greater than our present realities and be willing to go the distance to see it through.

Second, they stood together. Reading the text, we do not see anywhere that there was one spokesperson. The text does not single out one of the sisters or differentiate who singly spoke up. By doing this, the Scripture emphasizes that they were of one mind, one purpose, and most of all: one voice. They all received notable mention because they were all willing to stand together.

Third, they refused to settle for less. They said they wanted an inheritance "among our father's brothers" (Numbers 27:4). This means that they were not asking for a lesser portion but for full inclusion in the inheritance of their father. When going after your purpose, vision, and dreams, never settle for less than your worth, but that's the key – you must know your worth. You are valuable, loved, and worthy in the eyes of God. And just as the five sisters had the validation and approval of God, know that God's final say is validation enough for you to move forward in your God-given purpose and endeavors.

Prayer: *Loving God, thank you that in Your eyes I am worthy and loved. As I envision a world and reality greater than the one I see for myself and those coming after me, I pray for the courage, patience, and fortitude to forge ahead* *and see the vision through to the end. Thank you for the support you are gracing me with for this journey, knowing that You have the final say in my life, and it is all the validation I need. In the Name of Jesus the Christ, Amen.*

Put it into Practice: Is there something that you have always been afraid to try or do? Name it, commit it to prayer, and begin making measurable steps towards accomplishing it.

Notes

_____
_____
_____
_____
_____
_____
_____
_____
_____
_____
_____
_____
_____
_____
_____
_____
_____
_____
_____
_____

Notes

JANUARY 2nd
Vashti
"Drawing the Line"

Background Reading: Esther 1:1-2:4

"But Queen Vashti refused to come at the king's bidding..." (Esther 1:12a, NET)

There would be no story of Esther without Vashti. A woman who knew the power and dignity of the word, "No." While we are not given her motives for refusing, we are given the reason for the king's request in Esther 1:10-11, "On the seventh day, as King Ahasuerus was feeling the effects of the wine, he ordered...to bring Queen Vashti into the king's presence wearing her royal high turban. He wanted to show the people and the officials her beauty, for she was very attractive." (Esther 1:10-11, NET) With this drunken command, Vashti refused to be objectified and used for optics, to stroke the king's ego, for the people's amusement and amazement, or to prove a point. She was the first to embody the risk-taking "If I perish, I perish" spirit that Esther would give voice to in chapter 4 verse 16, and even though we don't hear Vashti's voice in the text, hers was the refusal heard around the world.

When we stand up to ungodly power structures, unethical demands, or refuse to be used as pawns in someone else's game, we can rest assured that we will make waves, and there will be consequences. For Vashti, that meant being deposed (which could have meant death). For us, it may mean loss of social standing, a smaller circle, being less liked, rejection from those we hold dear, having to make career changes, just to name a few. Even though Vashti's story leaves us with unanswered questions about her fate, it was her "no" that paved the way for Esther's story. How many women's shoulders do we stand upon today that refused to be used, run-over, and objectified, even when it meant deep sacrifice?

Indeed, Vashti bears witness that your "no" will cost you something, but not as much as sacrificing your morality, dignity, and identity in Christ. But know that with every no, there is a counterbalancing "yes." Yes, to hold your head up high. Yes, to the new path that God is carving out for you. Yes, to the new blessings, relationships, and opportunities that your bravery and faith will now bring, and most of all, yes to paving the way for someone else's story to unfold.

Prayer: *Wonderful God, I thank you that I am fearfully and wonderfully made in Your image. Because I was created on purpose, I ask for the strength to continue to walk in that purpose and the resilience to never accept anything less. I receive the courage that I need to say "no" to toxic relationships, associations, and activities that seek to diminish who you have created me to be. Today I say "yes" to the path and new adventures you have laid out for me. I give you praise for those whose stories will be able to unfold because of my courage to say "no" to what is dishonorable and "yes" to what you have called me to. In the Name of Jesus the Christ, Amen.*

Put it into Practice: Take the week ahead and ask God to reveal any areas of your life where you need to draw boundaries or toxicity that you need to walk away from. Ask God for the courage and strategy to mark and maintain healthy boundaries, then take the appropriate steps to activate those boundaries.

Notes

Notes

JANUARY 3rd
Lois & Eunice
"A Faith Handed On"

Background Reading: 2 Timothy 1:1-14

I recall your sincere faith that was alive first in your grandmother Lois and in your mother Eunice, and I am sure is in you. (2 Timothy 1:5, NET)

In a reflective letter to Timothy, Paul speaks words of encouragement reminding him to be strong, hold on to what he has been taught, and faithfully walk out his calling. What is striking is that at the very beginning of his words, even before he mentions what he has imparted into Timothy, he admonishes Timothy to ground himself for the future in the faith exemplified by his grandmother and mother.

When we think of what our mothers and their mothers before them passed on to us, we tend to think of secret recipes, perhaps a certain laugh, eye color, or temperament. Or maybe we think of things that were passed onto us that weren't so good that we spend our lives trying to escape or not live into. But imagine being the recipient of such a legacy of faith that it is recognizable and identifiable in your own life. Imagine being told, "You have faith just like your grandmother and your mother!"

What faith these two women must have possessed! So much so that their faith was remarkable enough to be recognized as a hallmark of Timothy's life. They understood how important the things we hand down are.

They gave Timothy a legacy beyond antiques and heirlooms, but one of the eternal things that would carry him in trying times. They took seriously the Scriptures that reminded Israel in Deuteronomy 6:6-7 (NET): "These words I am commanding you today must be kept in mind, and you must teach them to your children and speak of them as you sit in your house, as you walk along the road, as you lie down, and as you get up."

Never underestimate the strength of the prayers, love, and faith that you have deposited in your children and those around you. We don't know if Lois and Eunice lived to see the man of God that Timothy became, but we do know that their faith and deposit in Timothy bore fruit for generations to come, even now. You never know how the seeds of faith that you are sowing into your children will bear fruit, and while you may not live to see the full impact of your faith in others' lives, be encouraged. God is faithful, and your labor is not and will not be in vain. Your prayers and faith have no expiration date.

Prayer: *Loving God, thank you for the faith that has been deposited in me by Holy Spirit. As you lead me, I pray for resilience in sowing seeds of faith to those in my sphere of influence. I pray that in the moments when I get discouraged because the fruit of those seeds seems to be small or non-existent, that you would remind me that your work in people's lives has no expiration date. Thank You that You are Lord of the harvest, and in due time, you will give the increase to those seeds. In the Name of Jesus the Christ, Amen.*

Put into Practice: Take time today to give thanks to God for those who played a positive role in your spiritual formation. If able, reach out to them and express appreciation for the ways they have blessed your life.

Notes

Notes

JANUARY 4th
Mary of Bethany, Sister of Martha and Lazarus
"True Discipleship"

Background Reading: John 12:1-11

"Then Mary took three quarters of a pound of expensive aromatic oil from pure nard and anointed the feet of Jesus. She then wiped his feet dry with her hair. (Now the house was filled with the fragrance of the perfumed oil.) So Jesus said, 'Leave her alone. She has kept it for the day of my burial.'" (John 12:3,7, NET)

John 12 closes out what many Biblical scholars call the "Book of Signs" in the Gospel of John. The chapters that remain comprise the "Book of Glory," which focuses on the suffering, death, and resurrection of Jesus. In this transitional chapter, we find Mary of Bethany, who interrupts a dinner party to anoint Jesus's feet.

This act by Mary was by no means a wasteful display of honor, as deemed by Judas. In fact, John's Gospel is careful to tell us that this dinner occurs six days before Passover. What's significant about this is that typically this would have been the day that the Jews chose the Passover lamb for the feast and would anoint its legs and feet with oil. So, Jesus Himself understands very well the importance of what she is doing – anointing Him as the sacrificial Passover Lamb.

Although Mary was not named among "The Twelve," she shows us what it means to be a true disciple. In two instances of her mention in Scripture, here in John, and in Luke 10:38-42, she postures herself at Jesus' feet. Being at one's feet was indicative of submitting to a person's teaching as their disciple. Further, even more so than those who walked so closely with Him, Mary seems to be the only one in the room which is acutely mindful of Jesus's assignment that looms nearby. By anointing His feet, on such a significant day, she brings the focus of the people in the room, and us, back to the fact that Jesus is not just the One who does extraordinary miracles, but that His greatest miracle yet, His self-sacrificing love, lay just ahead.

Indeed, a true disciple doesn't just focus on the Jesus who saved the day at the wedding in Cana or even the Jesus who can bring the dead back to life. A true disciple never loses focus of the heart of mission and message of Jesus and the Gospel: "No one has greater love than this—that one lays down his life for his friends." (John 15:13, NET). How fitting then that the anointing of Jesus by Mary, a true disciple, is the last signpost in the Book of Signs, ultimately pointing us towards Jesus's glory, His demonstrated love for all of us.

Prayer: Loving God, thank you for the ways that you demonstrate Your love and care for us and all of creation. Thank You for Jesus Christ, who showed us the way of love in the most tangible way possible. We ask that You help us be faithful disciples, followers of The Way, that always point back to the self-sacrificing love of Jesus and remain humble at His feet. In the Name of Jesus the Christ, Amen.

Put it into Practice: Set some time aside today/this week to think about what being a disciple of Jesus has meant in your life and what it means to you today. In what ways are you sensing the call to "sit at Jesus's feet" today/this week?

Notes

Notes

JANUARY 5th
Leah
"Readjust Your Focus"

Background Reading: Genesis 29:1-30:24

She became pregnant again and had another son. She said, 'This time, I will praise the Lord.' That is why she named him Judah. Then she stopped having children.
(Genesis 29:25, NET)

Leah, with the "delicate" eyes, had no say in so many matters. No say in her marriage to Jacob. She couldn't even stop her heart from loving him when all of his love went to her sister Rachael instead of her. With so many things in her life out of her control, she hedged her bet on the one thing that she knew she could do – birth babies – in hopes of her husband's love in return. Even the names of her first three children reflected that unrequited longing. But, something happened when she gave birth to Judah, her fourth child. When she gave birth to Judah, she chose to put her focus and hope elsewhere for a moment in her life. She said, "This time, I will praise the Lord." This time, the baby wasn't all about Jacob or earning his love. This time, she decided that God was enough. She would now fix her gaze on the one that had seen her estate and opened her womb in the first place. "And it was the child named solely in ode to God, not Jacob, who produced kings and queens and eventually produced the lineage of the Messiah."

As women, how many times have we given of ourselves, body and soul, to relationships, jobs, and other endeavors, only to find that what we produced still didn't yield the results we had hoped? Like Leah, we say to ourselves, "Maybe *this* opportunity, *this* job, *this* relationship will be different," only to find that the cycle of frustration, hurt, and discouragement continues. However, when we decide, like Leah, to fix our gaze on the Gift-Giver alone, it is then that we can produce lasting fruit, even out of painful circumstances.

Now, while we would love for Leah's story to end with her being free of this cycle of jealousy and desire, we find that she gets caught back up in a losing battle for Jacob's love once again with her sister. Her story is a sobering reminder that cycles are more difficult to break than we would like to admit. But, I believe that if she were here today, she would lovingly cheer us on towards walking a different path and our own freedom, which is possible with perseverance, faith, and focus.

Prayer: *Loving God, thank you for being the God of the breakthrough. I admit that, at times, I have allowed my focus to be guided by dysfunctional and toxic mental and emotional strongholds instead of your love. I ask that you set me free from any unhealthy cycles relating to myself, You, and others. Recalibrate and realign my focus to be divinely guided and centered. I declare that Your Spirit lives in me, and because there is freedom where your Spirit is, I declare and affirm that I am free. Free to live and free to love. In the Name of Jesus the Christ, amen!*

Put it into Practice: Today is a day of sacred analepsis and prolepsis! Reflect on and give thanks for the ways that God has helped you overcome unhealthy patterns and cycles in your life, and allow those testimonies to be faith anchors as you ask God to bring to your attention any unhealthy patterns or cycles that need to be broken in your life now. Seek and trust God to give you the strategy and the courage to break free from those patterns and cycles.

Notes

Notes

JANUARY 6th
Hagar
"The Gift of Being Seen"

Background Reading: Genesis 16 and Genesis 21

"So Hagar named the Lord who spoke to her, 'You are the God who sees me,' for she said, 'Here I have seen one who sees me!' That is why the well was called Beer Lahai Roi." (Genesis 16:13-14a, NET)

Hagar was an outsider -- she was a slave, a foreigner, and a woman. To top it off, she found herself in the middle of a messy drama: pregnant, distressed, and in the middle of nowhere. Yet, in the middle of a mess and the middle of nowhere, she has a personal encounter with God, the Living One. Isn't it amazing how God can still locate us, no matter how messy or desolate the place we are in life? Until now, the stars of this Biblical drama have been Abraham and Sarah, but in a world where she would have been overlooked, a blip on a radar, Hagar's story is all about how God sees those in the margins. And this is not just a passing encounter. Even her mistress Sarah has not yet had the privilege of personally speaking to the Living One. But God chooses to say, give instruction, and make a promise to her and assure her that her legacy on the earth is secure.

There was a well built at the place where she saw God and God saw her: a powerful moment of mutual seeing between Hagar and the Divine. There are three main responses in Scripture from people encountering God: offerings, memorials (like a rock memorial), and wells. Hagar's story gives us the first mention of a well in Scripture. This well would be a physical, tangible reminder for generations of the encounter between this non-Israelite, Egyptian slave woman and God. Wells are deep places, and there will be those experiences of God that will make such a profound impact on us that they will be like wells out of which we can draw in times of distress and discouragement. These memory wells of God-moments are powerful, and our ability to recall the faithfulness of God in trying times is invaluable and provides us with hope (Lamentations 3:21-26).

While the Angel of the Lord mentions her being heard, Hagar focuses on seeing and being seen. Us being drawn to these senses and into Hagar's story reminds us that God both hears the voice of the voiceless, and God sees the overlooked among us. May our spirits ever be drawn back to the well of knowing that the Living One is mindful of us.

Prayer: *O God, The Living One, thank You that Your mindfulness of us always prompts You to act graciously towards us and on our behalf. Thank You for seeing us. Thank You for hearing us. Thank You for allowing us to encounter You even in the wilderness and messiness of our journey. Remind us in the times when we feel unseen, unnoticed, and unheard that we can return to the well of Your faithfulness to us and find comfort, strength, and rest. In the Name of Jesus the Christ, Amen.*

Put it into Practice: Think about an encounter with God that made a profound and defining impact on your life. In what ways did that encounter change your life? Write this encounter down, or pick up a trinket that symbolizes that experience and put it in a place where you can refer back to it in challenging times for encouragement.

Notes

Notes

Notes

Author's Bio

Passionate about education, Jamie is a fourth-generation ordained Christian minister and educator dedicated to providing opportunities for people to learn how to be whole while positively impacting their families, communities, and the world.

Jamie is a graduate of The Johns Hopkins University, Wesley Theological Seminary, and The Catholic University of America, holding undergraduate and graduate degrees in Near Eastern Studies, Divinity, and Biblical Studies.

With over 20 years of experience in ministry, leadership, and education, Jamie specializes in teaching, learning, and leading in ministry and academic settings. She is most fulfilled when she can serve both the academic and church communities.

Jamie is the founder and visionary of Jamie Coles Burnette Ministries, a teaching ministry focused on inviting people into life with God through Jesus Christ and helping them build lives according to Godly principles. She also happily shares her life with her beloved husband, Elliot.

Her life bears witness to the words of Jesus that: "…with God, all things are possible," and she lives daily in gratitude for that being a reality in her life.

Connections

For bulk purchases, speaking engagements, and/or comments, please connect with me on my social media outlets, email, or website at:

Rev. Jamie Burnette
Soul Sabbath Ministries
Email: hello@soulsabbathliving.love
Ministry Website: www.soulsabbathliving.love

www.ingramcontent.com/pod-product-compliance
Lightning Source LLC
Chambersburg PA
CBHW050706160426
43194CB00010B/2024